AF413532

OH NO! ZEUS ATE HIS WIFE!

Mythology and Folklore
Children's Greek & Roman Books

Speedy Publishing LLC

40 E. Main St. #1156

Newark, DE 19711

www.speedypublishing.com

Copyright 2017

Zeus was the god of justice, thunder, lightning and the sky and his symbols included the bull, the eagle, the oak tree, and the lightning bolt. Yes, according to Greek mythology, he did swallow his wife. In this book, you will learn about this interesting Greek god.

Who was Zeus?

Zeus, whose Roman name was Jupiter, lived on Mount Olympus as the king of the Greek gods and his wife was the goddess Hera. His parents were Rhea and Cronus and his children were Ares, Athena, Apollo, Artemis, Aphrodite, Dionysus, Hermes, Heracles, Helen of Troy and Hephaestus.

ZEUS

What Were His Powers?

Zeus had many powers and was known as the most powerful Greek god. His ability to throw bolts of lightning was his most famous power. Pegasus, his winged horse, would carry the lightning bolts and Zeus trained an eagle for retrieving the bolts. He also had control over the weather and had the ability to cause rain and large storms.

Zeus had many other powers that included the ability to mimic other people's voices and shape shift which would make him look like another person or an animal. If someone would make him angry, he would sometimes use his powers to turn them into animal for punishment.

HADES

Who Were Zeus' Sisters and Brothers?

His sisters and brothers also were gods and goddesses that each had powers of their own. Of his three brothers, he was the youngest and he held the most power. Hades, who was his oldest brother, ruled over the Underworld. Poseidon, who was his other brother, was god over the seas. His three sisters included Demeter, Hestia, and Hera, who became his wife.

The Children of Zeus

Zeus had many children, some which were Olympic gods, including Ares, Apollo, Artemis, Athena, Aphrodite, Hermes and Dionysus. Additionally, he had children that were half human and some that were heroes, including Perseus and Hercules. Some of Zeus' other children include the Graces, the Muses, and Helen of Troy.

APOLLO

STATUE OF ZEUS AT OLYMPIA

Zeus - King of the Gods

He was born as the sixth child to Rhea and Cronus, who were Titan gods. Cronus, his father, ate the first five of his children since he was worried they might become too powerful. Even though they didn't die, they were not able to get out of his stomach. Once Zeus was born, his mother, Rhea, hid him from Cronus so that Cronus would not able to eat him too. Zeus ended up being raised by the Nymphs in the forest.

As he grew older, Zeus hoped to rescue his sisters and brothers. He obtained a potion and was able to disguise himself so that his father wouldn't know who he was. Cronus then drank the special potion and his five children were coughed up. These five children were Hera, Demeter, Hestia, Poseidon, and Hades.

STATUE OF ZEUS IN FOUNTAIN, PIAZZA NAVONA, ROME, ITALY

CYCLOPES GIANT

The Titans and Cronus were angered and battled Zeus and his siblings for many years. For assistance with the fighting, Zeus set the giants free, as well as the Cyclopes of Earth. They supplied the Olympians weapons for use in battle with the Titans. Hades got a helm which made him invisible, Poseidon received a trident, and Zeus received lightning and thunder. The Titans went on to surrender and Zeus had them locked deep into the underground.

It was then Mother Earth's turn and she became angry at Zeus for placing the Titans underground. She then sent the Typhon, who was known to be the most fearsome monster around the world, to battle the Olympians. Even though the other Olympians ran and hid, Zeus did not. He remained, fighting the Typhon and trapping him below Mount Etna, and this became the legend of how Mount Etna turned into a volcano.

MOUNTAIN ETNA, SICILY

Zeus had now become the most powerful over all of the gods. Along with his fellow gods, he moved on to live at Mount Olympus. It was there that he married Hera and became ruler over all gods as well as humans.

Greek Mythology

The Greeks had several gods and many myths and stories that went along with them. It consisted of the tales and stores about the Greek goddesses, heroes, and gods. Since the Greeks constructed temples and tendered sacrifices to their main gods, it came to be the religion of Ancient Greece.

CHRONOS VS ZEUS, POSEIDON AND HADES

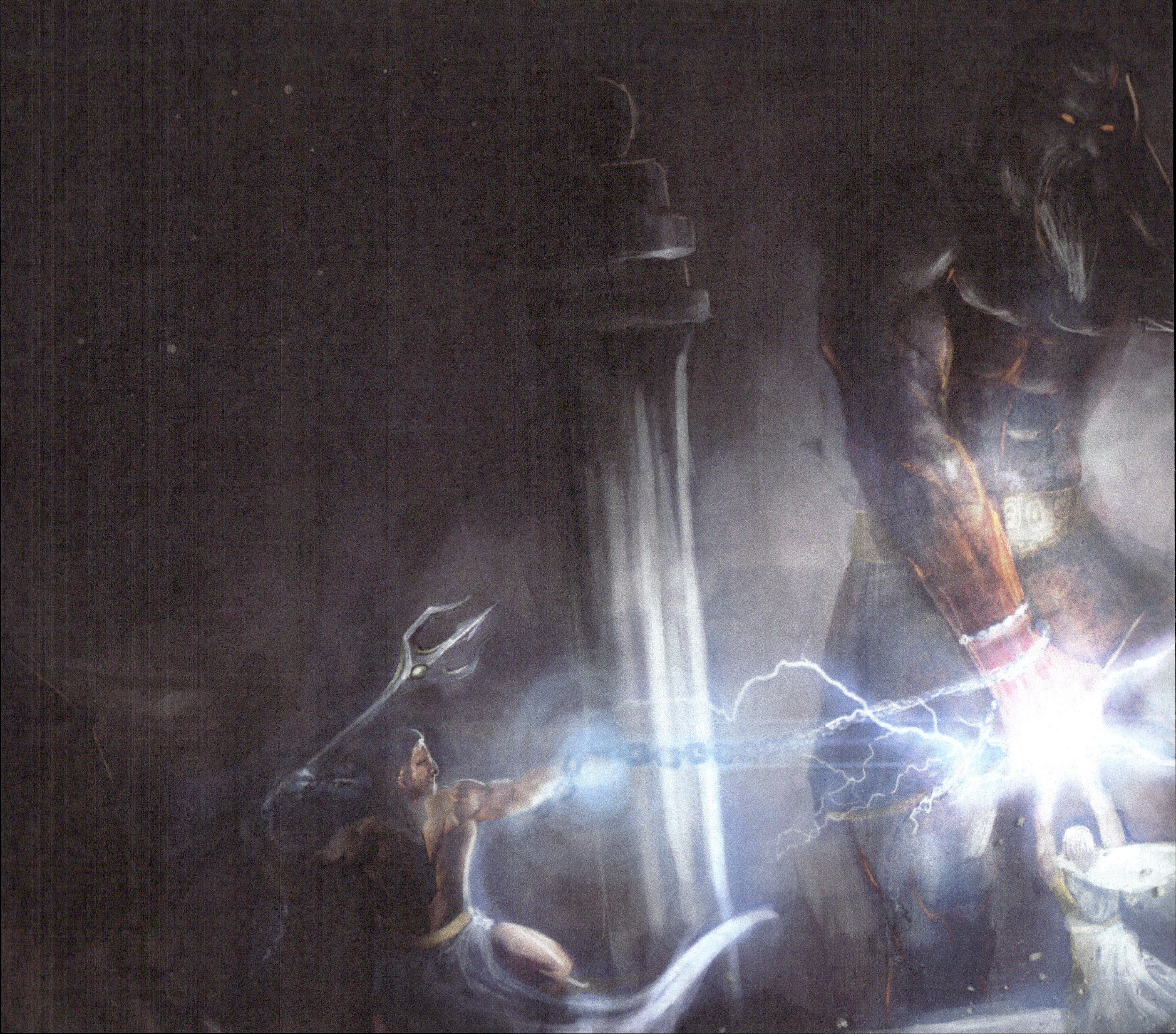

A few of the major Greek Gods are listed here:

THE TITANS

These were the elder (first) gods. The twelve included Zeus' parents, Rhea and Cronus and ruled during the golden age and were later overtaken by their children, who were led by Zeus.

CRONUS: He is the god of time and Titans' leader.

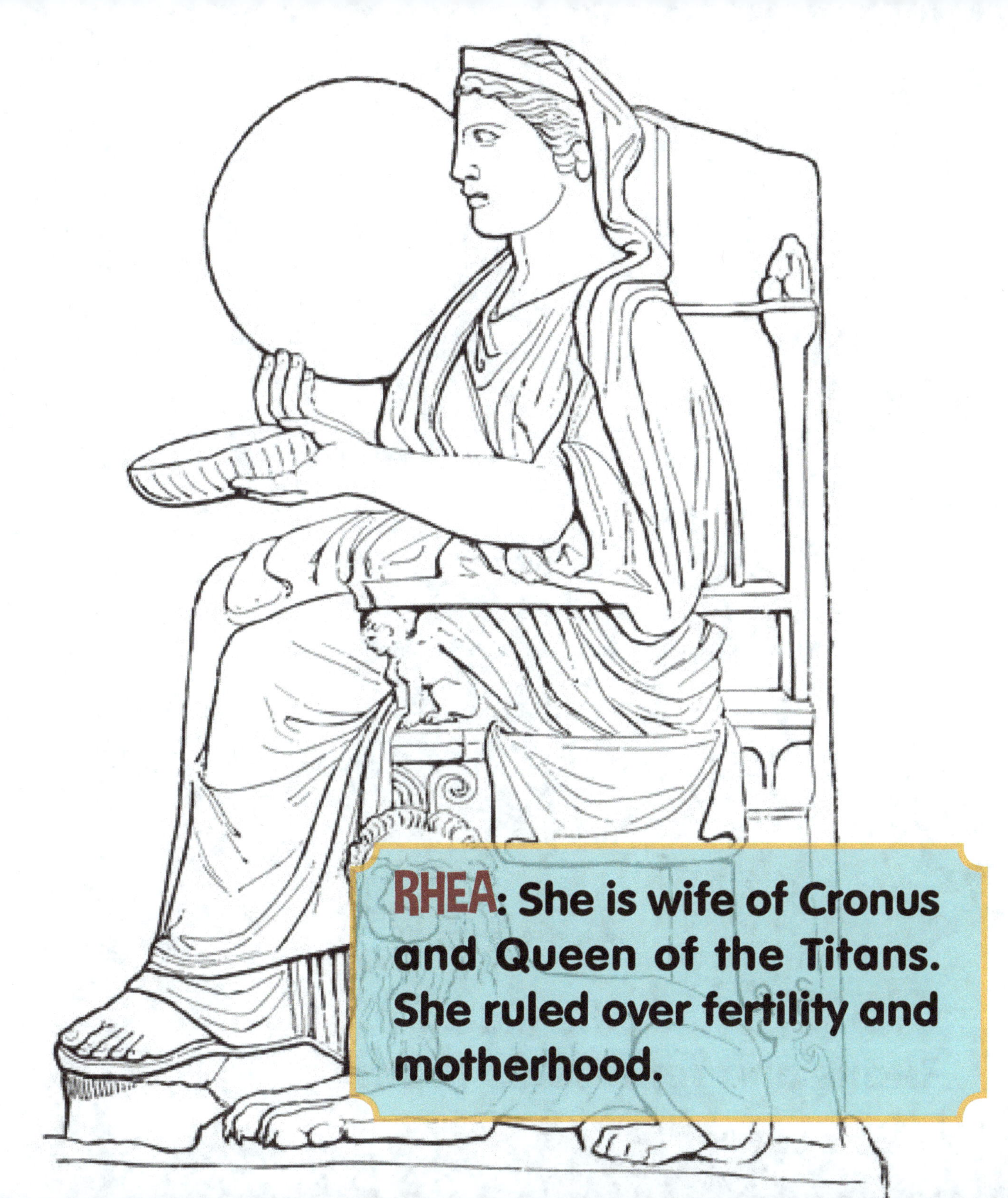

RHEA: She is wife of Cronus and Queen of the Titans. She ruled over fertility and motherhood.

OCEANUS: He is the eldest of all of the Titans and represents the sea.

TETHYS: She is known to be the goddess of the sea and the wife of Oceanus.

HYPERION: He is known as the Titan of light and the father to Helios, the sun god.

THEIA: She is the wife of Hyperion and is the goddess of shining and brightness.

HELIOS

SCULPTURE OF LETO

COEUS: He is known as Titan of the stars and intelligence.

PHOEBE: She is the mother to Leto and the Goddess of intelligence and brightness.

MNEMOSYNE: She is the mother to Muses (Zeus was Muses' father) and represents memory for Greek mythology.

THEMIS: She is the mother of Hours and Fates (their father was Zeus) and she overrules law and order.

CRIUS: He is known as the Titan of the constellations.

LAPETUS: He is the god of mortality and fathered many of the more powerful Titan children that included Prometheus and Atlas.

The Olympians

There were twelve Olympian gods and they were known as the major gods of the Greeks. They resided on Mount Olympus.

ZEUS: He is the known leader over the Olympians and god of lighting and sky. The lightning bolt is his symbol and he married his sister, Hera.

HERA: She is queen of the gods and is married to Zeus. She is the goddess of family and marriage. The lion, the pomegranate, the cow, and the peacock were her symbols.

POSEIDON: He is god of the earthquakes, ocean, and horses and the trident are his symbol. He is brother to Hades and Zeus.

DIONYSUS: He is the lord of celebrations and wine and patron god to art and the theatre. The grapevine is his symbol. Zeus is his father, and Dionysus is the youngest Olympian.

APOLLO: He is the Greek god of music, light, prophecy, and archery. The lyre, the bow and arrow, and the sun are his symbols. He has a twin sister named Artemis.

ARTEMIS: She goddess of archery, animals, and the hunt. The bow and arrow, the moon, and the deer are her symbols. She has a twin brother named Apollo.

HERMES: He is the god of thieves and commerce in addition to being messenger for the gods. His symbols consist of the winged sandals and the caduceus. His son, Pan, is god of nature.

ATHENA: She is the Greek goddess of defense, war, and wisdom. Her symbols consist of the olive branch and the owl and she is also Athens' patron god.

ARES: He is the god of war and the spear and the shield are his symbols. Hera and Zeus are his parents.

APHRODITE: She is goddess of love and beauty and the swan, the rose, and the dove are her symbols. She was married to the God Hephaestus.

HEPHAESTUS: He is god of fire and works as a blacksmith and a craftsman to the gods. The hammer, the donkey, the anvil, and fire are his symbols. His wife is Aphrodite.

DEMETER: She is goddess of the seasons and agriculture and her symbols include the pig and wheat.

HADES: He is god of the Underworld. While he lives in the Underworld, rather than at Mount Olympus, he is still referred to as a god of the Olympians.

Greek Heroes

Greek heroes were considered to be strong and brave men favored by the gods. They would perform brave adventures and exploits. Even as a mortal, the heroes would somehow be related to the gods.

HERCULES: He is son to Zeus and known as the most amazing hero in Greek Mythology. He had several labors that he had to perform and was quite strong, fighting several monsters during his adventures.

ACHILLES: He is the Trojan war's greatest hero as he was invincible, other than his heel. He is portrayed in Homer's Iliad as the central character.

ODYSSEUS: He is the hero of the Odyssey, Homer's epic poem. He was quite strong and brave, however, he got by mostly using his intelligence and wits.

ZEUS AND OTHER GREEK GODS AND GODDESSES

Greek mythology has so many interesting stories of gods and goddesses and their unique prowess. It is just one of the many attributes that Greece possess. Learning about Ancient Greece is truly fascinating!

For additional information you can visit your local library, research the internet, and ask questions of your teachers, family and friends.